Finding the Best Affiliate Products to Promote

Ensure your success with the right product to market.

IQ PRESS, INC.

Disclaimer

The Publisher has strived to be as accurate and complete as possible in the creation of this report, notwithstanding the fact that it does not warrant or represent at any time that the contents within are accurate due to the rapidly changing nature of the Internet.

The Publisher will not be responsible for any losses or damages of any kind incurred by the reader whether directly or indirectly arising from the use of the information found in this report.

This report is not intended for use as a source of legal, business, accounting or financial advice. All readers are advised to seek services of competent professionals in legal, business, accounting, and finance field.

No guarantees of income are made. Reader assumes responsibility for use of information contained herein. The author reserves the right to make changes without notice. The Publisher assumes no responsibility or liability whatsoever on the behalf of the reader of this report.

CONTENTS

ACKNOWLEDGMENTS

IQ Press, Inc. is a small publishing company dedicated to providing access to educational materials primarily in small business start-up and development. Their mission is to bring the reader useful information that can be implemented with a small capital outlay and generate income streams for the reader to implement.

We hope you enjoy these reports and that they will help improve your life.

www.IQPress.org

1 - INTRODUCTION

Finding the Best Affiliate Products to Promote

The Internet has become a virtual world. There is nothing that you can do in the real world that you cannot do in the virtual world including buying and selling products. This has been a known fact for some time, and when you promote products on the net it is called Internet marketing.

There are a number of websites that sell products and a few large organizations that dominate the market. Companies like Amazon and eBay are probably the best known names although there are others as well.

While Amazon and eBay sell products, they do not actively advertise them. Considering their sales volume and growth – Amazon grew 16% last year when compared to 2.4% for retail sales - it is possible that they feel that they do not need to advertise. Yet everyone knows the value of advertising. This gave birth to what is called the affiliate websites. When you are selling a product, and someone comes to you and tells you that they are willing to promote your product, they are vendors. When they do this online, they are called affiliates.

Affiliate marketing works because it is a win-win situation for both parties. The affiliate takes it upon themself to promote his website. He toils hard and puts in a lot of effort to increase his ranking on Google. The result is that any product that he is promoting for you will also get the increased exposure, and you have not spent one dime, or one minute of your time to do this.

The affiliate is paid a commission that can range anywhere from 4% to 30% of sales price depending on the product they are marketing. He is paid only if any person he directs to your site makes a purchase. The sales commission becomes your only cost to market and is fixed.

You keep track of which customer comes from which affiliate by giving each of your affiliates a different cookie or ID. This cookie has a definite expiration date and is installed in the system of any person who visits the affiliate 's site.
When the customer comes to you, the cookie in his system will tell you who has sent him there allowing you to keep track of both the number of people he directs to your site and the number of sales made. Most of this is automated and it is a system that works for everyone.

If instead of being the person who sells the product you are the affiliate, the process is the same, but in reverse. You contact the seller, get his cookie, and you are set. All you need to do is to put in the legwork to increase your web traffic because that is the basis of all conversions and ultimately the amount of money you can make.

Because you go to such lengths, investing your hard-earned money and time promoting a product, you need to make sure that the product that you choose is the right one. There are millions of products being sold online, but not all of them will give you what you are looking for. Then there are the scam artists who are out to cheat you.

This being the case you need to be careful how you choose the product that you want to market. There are a few ways to do this and we will discuss them in detail below.

Chapter 2 - Where do you start?

This is the first thing that you have to think of. Either you will be creating a completely new website or blog to market a specific product, or you will be integrating it into your existing site. There are pros and cons to both of these.

Promoting products on an existing site

If you already have a website or a blog up and running, you already have a certain ranking with Google. You can focus your attention on your one site and over time raise your ranking with all search engines. The advantage of this model is that you already have a certain amount of traffic that you are getting on a daily or weekly basis; this increases the chance of you getting a sale quickly.

In addition, if you have more than one product on your site, even if you only promote one product, all the other products will reap the benefit. You just have to concentrate on improving the ranking of your one site so that you increase traffic. Once you do this, if you have made a good choice on the products and if you have designed your web page well, the sales will come.

Naturally, you will have to pick and choose the kind of products that you promote. For example, if you have a website that reviews dishwashers, you don't want to try to start selling air conditioners there. You can take your pick of any dishwasher or accessory to promote, but you are pretty much limited to that one product category.

Of course, you can try to work around this by creating a generalized website where you can promote anything you like. The problem with that is that such sites have no focus at all. If you want to sell home appliances, beauty products, herbal medicines and books all in the same place, you will have to choose a name that is very generic, like "Amazon.com" for example. Unfortunately, it also takes that much more work to bring it to the notice of search engines first and then to the notice of the public.

When a person is looking to purchase anything online, he or she is apt to click on the link that carries the name of the product that they wish to buy. For example, if you name your site www.xyzreview.com people will realize that your site is providing reviews about the product xyz. If on the other hand you name your site www.purchaseproductsonline.com

nobody knows if you are connected in any way to the product xyz and may not click on it. Furthermore, even the search engines will lower your ranking because they tend to give the highest ranking to those sites that carry the search string in the site name itself.

Building separate sites for different products

This is the second option open to affiliates. They can choose to create different niche websites and then actively push their product online so that over time they get a good ranking with search engines, resulting in increased sales.

This tactic is a good option in that everything about it is a positive. You can choose a site name that carries the keyword in the name of the site itself. As mentioned previously, sites that carry the keyword in their address not only have a better chance of ranking highly, but are also the ones that are clicked on more frequently.

You will be targeting a certain product and can focus your attention on that single product, helping you build a good site, one of the prerequisites to getting traffic. Online consumers will only stay and read what you have written if the site looks nice and if the content is worth reading. By focusing on a single product, you are able to provide targeted content, what people are looking for. This increases your conversion ratio.

On the other hand, you will have to create a different site for every product that you promote. This will increase your work a hundred fold because instead of having one site where you can sell five different products, you will have five sites selling one product each. This means that if you want to sell a total of five products, you will have to create five different websites, and work on all of them so that they all start generating income streams for you.

It is a little difficult to decide what to do, and many people prefer to go the latter way, creating different sites for different products, because even though it is more work, it gives you more returns. This is the most common advice that you get with regards to affiliate marketing.

Focus is everything and if you do not target one thing, a niche or a product, you cannot hit anything. Yet, this is not always the case because if you create a generalized site but are willing to work on it for some time, like Amazon you are creating a brand, and over time people will start to recognize the brand. Once this happens, the sky is the limit on what you can promote.

Amazon.com is a simple case in point. The company was started in 1006, but did not show any profit until tho fourth quarter of 2001. At that time profits were a modest $5 million on a turnover of nearly $1 billion. Now, just nine years later, it is growing at a rapid 14% while retail sales are struggling to post 2.5% growth. Their profits have grown to more than $2.4 billion, and are still growing. Yet, it is important to note that it took six years for them to become profitable.

Chapter 3 - Where do you look for products to promote?

Once you have the first question out of the way, it is time to start looking for the products to promote. This is really not as easy as many people say it is and requires a lot of effort. There are not too many places where you can look for products and most of them are known. Below we will take each of these and individually discuss their pros and cons.

Google AdSense

This is one of the easiest ways to spot products to sell. Whenever you type out any search string, you will get sponsored ads on the right hand side of the page. Usually these ads would have been put up by affiliates wanting to increase traffic to their websites.

For example, if you type in "Herbal beauty creams" in the search bar, you will get five ads on the right hand side of the results page. Barring one, all the others are affiliate sites that sell different kinds of herbal beauty products, and just looking at the different products they sell will start you off on your search for products to market.

Generally, if you follow the link to the home page, you will find details of how to become an affiliate member. It is not necessary to sign up to the affiliate network immediately as there are many considerations you need to look at before you pick a product, but it does make finding them easier. The negative of this method is that you will be entering a crowded market. If there are four ads by affiliates themselves, think of the total number of affiliates who will be marketing these products.

Standing out from this crowd to make your site unique is not going to be easy. Yet, if a lot of affiliates are promoting a particular product it usually means that it is selling well, so the chances of you making a sale are also better.

Check out your competition

This is one of the easiest ways to find products. If you are in a niche, you will be aware of whom your competitors are, and all you have to do is to follow their lead. This way is easy because you let someone else do all the legwork for you, while all you have to do is copy them. There is a lot of analysis required before you decide on whether you want to go with a product or not, and allowing another person to do this frees you up to do other work.

The drawback to this model is that you are always following the leader. Depending on how long it takes you to set up your site, get content posted with everything else you have to do to get its ranking up, you may very well miss the boat. However, some people follow this policy because their costs are low. All they have to worry about is marketing a product, not finding it.

Use affiliate programs

There are a number of affiliate programs like Google's affiliate network and ClickBank that allow you to browse through sites that have registered with them and who are using affiliates. It is similar to what you do with the Google results page ads, but you get a much larger number of sites from which to choose. You can search according to product or niche and identify the product you want to go with.

Not only this, you will be able to compare the commission given to affiliates. Different sites will offer different percentages of commission, and while going with the one that offers the highest commission may seem like a good idea, it may also mean that the high commission is because of the difficulty in selling the product. A more easily salable one may have a lower commission per sale, but total sales volume could be much greater, giving you more total income.

The biggest advantage is not even this. Most of these affiliate programs will give you a track record of the company that you want to start marketing for. This is very important because if you are pulled in by a scam artist, sell his products and he doesn't pay you, there is very little you can do about it. Checking the track record of various sites gives you the knowledge that you require to weed out the strong candidates from the not so strong.

You can check their payment history to see if they make their payments properly, and even check how long they have been online. Generally speaking, going with someone who has had a web presence for at least 6 months to a year is good; if not, you have no idea if they are real or not. By going with sites that already have an affiliate program running you may be entering an already tight market, but at least you know you will not be cheated.

Look up online stores

This is becoming very popular nowadays. Amazon actively encourages affiliates and with their sales volume increasing by leaps and bounds, it is relatively easy to make a sale on Amazon. Not only that, their whole affiliate marketing system is mostly automated and there are no payment issues with commissions.

There are a few negatives with Amazon offering the lowest commissions anywhere on the net. They start off at a low 4% and many times you will have to work really hard to start seeing any money from your site at all. Many affiliates just drop out because they are putting in more than they get out of it.

Yet, if you are willing to be patient it is also one of the best methods. Not only does Amazon give you all the details of what the most searched for products are on their site, they give you the option of tracking a number of other details. There are a number of people who earn just out of promoting products on Amazon. Their per product earning may not be much, averaging around $1000 per month for a really good affiliate program, but if you have 10 such sites you're earning quite a tidy sum of money.

Amazon has been taken simply as an example, and the same is true of any online store that you want to start marketing for. All of them know the value of affiliates. Many of them take a day to check into the antecedents of those who want to start on their affiliate program to find out of you are serious or not before accepting you into their program. Although there is no minimum qualification that you need to become an affiliate, it is better if you have an existing website with a bare minimum amount of traffic monthly. It shows that you are in it with your eyes open and for the long torm.

Approach potential partners

This is something that you can do only after you are really set up with a really good site and are doing business. You can approach both online partners and offline ones to check with them if they would be interested in having you market their products.

This will work only if you are able to offer an already existing marketing network, with both a large amount of traffic as well as sales going on in your site. Most companies are interested in increasing sales and are open to commissions if you can give actual increase in sales. A few of the top bloggers and review sites have done this with success, even approaching companies that have never done any online marketing before and partnering them.

Although this means that you already have an existing set up, if you can do this you are effectively putting yourself in a place where there is absolutely no competition. Because these companies themselves have never worked with affiliates in the past there is no competition that you have to worry about.

You would still have to do a basic analysis to find out if you have a good chance of making a sale or not. For example, if you are able to convince Ferrari or Lamborghini that you are a good person to start an affiliate program with, it still does not mean that you will be able to sell even one car. You need to research into the market to find such products that have a reasonably good chance of being sold online.

Google search

This is the simplest way for you to find anything that you are looking for. If you want to enter the health and fitness niche, just Googling "health and fitness" will give you a number of products. This is very time consuming, but there is nothing better to give you an impression of how the market is. In fact, if you rely only on affiliate programs and other directories, you will be missing out on a number of products whose manufacturers are not a part of these directories. They may not necessarily be against affiliates as such, just against being part of a third party program.

Even with all the amount of online activity that is going on, not every niche is crowded, and sometimes there may be a new product that has been launched in the market, and you will not find more than one or two sites promoting it. This is the opportunity for you to jump into that particular niche and take advantage of this lesser competition.

A simple example would be when it comes to record labels that come out. When a particular artist brings out an album, it does not take you more than 24 hours to find out how much of a hit it has become in the market. Checking online the next day will tell you what the competition is like and very often it will be nil. If you work fast, you can have your site up in just a couple of days at the most, to take advantage of the interest in the public for that album.

Getting affiliated and starting your marketing is going to be very easy simply because there is little competition. Getting to be the number 1 ranked site is very easy as long as you take some basic precautions like including it in your site's URL and putting in at least a couple of good quality content that is optimized towards that artist's name and other related keywords.

Interest may taper off within just a matter of weeks, but you would have taken advantage of the wave of public interest, and have ridden high on it because you got an early start.

How do you identify products to promote

After you have gone through some or all of the above-mentioned ways to identify products to market, your work is still not over. You are still left with choosing which product you want to go with. Using Amazon or Google's affiliate network may be very easy, but all that it will help you with is with giving you options to choose from. You still have to choose, and if you make the wrong choice you will not only be not earning any money, you will be wasting your time and effort on something that is well spent elsewhere.

Choosing these products is an art, you need to have a gut instinct for it. There are a number of tools that will help you with making the choice, and we will discuss them in detail later, but making the final choice is still something that is as arbitrary as you picking one because you like it. If picking products were totally scientific there would be no place for you to enter in at all because everyone else would use the same tools that you want to make use of and choose products to market. It is because it is not so easy, and it requires a lot of hard work that there is potential for the person who is willing to work hard at it.

There are a few basics to selling both online and offline that are applicable and the primary among this is that selling is very easy if you are catering to a need. For example, selling clothes is never difficult. What is difficult is to sell them at a 300% profit, because buyers know when they are being ripped off.

Most of the advice you get will be different variations of the same thing. Find something that people need and start to sell it. A slight tweak on the same thing would be to find things that people need, that other people do not sell, and then sell it. This is just to make your job of selling it much easier than it would be if there were a horde of others selling the same thing.

The problem is that most of the needs of people are already met. Not only that, there are a large number of sellers already in the market and finding a spot where you will be alone is going to be a difficult thing to do.

Taking advantage of changing trends will give you huge returns in a short time, but there is nothing permanent about it. You will have to keep finding new things to market and will always have to be on your toes.

It is simply because of all these difficulties that choosing the product to sell becomes an art. You make use of the tools available to you to gather as much information as you can about the product and then take a call on whether it is a good idea to promote it or not.

Below we will take a look at both what you can do as well as the tools available to you to help you choose the product to promote on your site.

Chapter 4 - Become an Expert

This takes a lot of time, and even more hard work. The Internet is amazing in that it basically creates a level playing field for everyone. It takes very little money to start a website of your own, and if you are not particular, you can even host your site for free at certain places.

This means that you have just as much of a chance as anyone else out there to make good. The bad thing is that this increases the competition tremendously. While in real life, it takes a lifetime of hard work to not only become an expert in a certain field, but to be accepted as such, it takes considerably less time online. Yet, this same factor means that there is no dearth of experts in any field on the net. You will therefore have to put in a lot of hard work to show people that you truly are an expert and that what you say is reliable. This is because most of these so-called experts are really not, and all they do is scrape information off other sites and put it on their own. It does not take long before people find out that such people rarely have an opinion of their own, and discard them.

The true expert though will not only catch the fancy of the internet public, but will stay there for a length of time, and even build up a fan following. Let us take a simple example to explain the point. If you are going to set yourself up as an expert on cameras, you will find that there are a number of affiliate sites that push products by saying the exact same thing, that they are experts on cameras.

However, you invest in some time to build your site up as a place where people can come to for reliable camera reviews, you will find that pretty soon there will be a number of people who do. As long as you make sure that your reviews are honest and accurate you are sure to become popular sooner rather than later.

If you start to sell cameras from your site, you are poised to take advantage of a lot of traffic that comes to your site looking for reviews. Even if most of them are only looking for the reviews but are not interested in making a purchase online, you will still profit from the few who do.

The reason why the reviews need to be accurate and honest is because if not, the same people who came to you thinking you were an expert will go out of their way to tell everyone else that you are a fraud. You will find bad reviews about your site cropping up all over the net, and all of a sudden you have lost everything you had.

This also means that you do not need to go searching for products to promote. Any new camera in the market that you do not have on your site is a potential candidate for promotion. There is little in the way of research or analysis that needs to be done, and all you have to do is to put in a review of the model and sit back.

The advantage of this model is that you have a regular income stream. Even if you have to perform a little maintenance work to always make sure that your content is current, or ensuring that you have a new model up on your site within a few days of launch, everything else runs along pretty smoothly.

The flip side though is that you will not be able to take advantage of anything new on the market other than cameras. If Apple brings out its new phone, you won't be able to do anything about it. Having a site that is too general is not good because you will not be able to focus on any one product or niche, bringing down the value of your whole site.

Online stores

Most affiliate sites go with the large online stores because not only is it easy to become an affiliate, it is also easier to sell the products. For example, if you have a site that promotes cameras, it is much easier to sell these cameras through Amazon or eBay than through some other site. With the number of scams only increasing, people are wary of making any sort of payment unless they know that the site is bona fide.

The second good thing is that most of these online stores really do not even give a good description of the product, far less a comparison with similar ones from other brands. This means that they are just a place where people can buy, but it also means that people who want to buy will look elsewhere for expert opinions. If you are the person with the expert opinion, they will visit you, and if you have been convincing enough, will purchase the product online thus crediting you with the sale.

For example, you have decided on washing machines as your niche; you will find that Amazon stocks pretty much everything that you can find in your local store, in terms of brands and models, and then some more.

You have two choices here, you can go with washing machines as a niche for your site, or you can target specific manufacturers or even brands to sell. The advantage of doing this is that you can focus more narrowly on a particular brand or model allowing you to get even higher in the search rankings.

Just looking through the most popular list on Amazon will tell you which model people are buying. Generally speaking, this alone is enough because if people are buying something, it means that there is a demand for the product. There are a few things that you have to do to confirm whether that particular model is what you want to promote.

Google it

This is the simplest way to check if the product you selected is already being marketed by other affiliates, and what kind of competition there is. If you see a number of paid advertisements as well as a number of affiliate sites coming up high in the display page, you know that this niche has already been covered and continue your search for your product.

The reason for this is obvious. You will be investing a lot of time, effort and money in building a site dedicated to a particular model and if you are going to have to fight it out, it will take you that much longer to start seeing any returns.

Going in for something where the competition is lesser is a better idea.

Probe your competition

This is the stage where most of us find ourselves. Most new niches are already taken and finding one where there is little to no competition is not as easy as it seems when you read about it. This means that you have to probe your competition to find out exactly how good they are.

For example, assume that you are interested in selling washing machines. You are pretty confident about selling them because you know there is a need for them. Everyone needs a washing machine. It only remains to be seen what the competition is like.

Searching on Google shows you that that particular niche is taken. There are a number of affiliate sites that deal with washing machines and some of them are actually quite popular and not only give you a good review of different washing machines, but also have a rating system that lets you compare different models.

If you search on Amazon for the bestselling washing machine, you will find that it is the Haier HLP23E. Yet, when you search with this "Haier HLP23E" as the search string, the results are completely different. You get six results in the display page and we will restrict ourselves to the first page alone.

In this first page, you will find that apart from Haier's official company site, there are six affiliate sites. Yet, out of these six there is only one that offers anything approaching a reasonable review of the product. Most of the other sites either give you a general description of the functioning of a washing machine, that you really don't want, or give you the features of the machine that you can get from the company site directly.

All the sites offer customer reviews, but barring one all the others have between two and five reviews, which is really not good. Even the one site that has what looks like a promising review by a customer looks like it has been written by a professional article writer rather than an actual user.

This research immediately shows you how you can improve on your competition. When you come down to this level, you will be able to identify products that have lesser competition than others. Yes it is not a totally empty niche, but there are possibilities that are worth exploring further.

Chapter 5 – Use tools

You will also find tools that supposedly help you find weaknesses in your competitor's websites. These tools are generally paid and will do everything from checking the keyword density to checking if your competitor has the ideal address in his URL.

The effectiveness of these tools is debatable, but then it is something additional that you can try if you want to. If you can do all the research yourself, it is probably the best, but where you cannot, you'll have to rely on tools, even if they are not as good.

The one thing that you need to remember is that all the pages that have made it to the first page on Google are those that have Haier HLP23E in the URL itself, which shows you how important it is to target specific products. Identifying products is all about legwork and although we have taken Amazon as the basis of our search, this can be done in many other ways.

Affiliate networks

ClickBank and Google's affiliate network gives you a list of all the products you can promote on your own site. All you have to do is to sign up with them, and this information is made available to you. The sign up procedure is free, and if you go through the procedure of finding products and marketing them, you find that it is one of the simplest there is.

You can search by product categories or you can go with specific keywords. If you want to go with the categories, you will get a list of all the products including the "vendor's pitch" which gives you relevant information about the product. This information may often not be enough, but it will at least help you shortlist likely products. You will have to do further research before you choose individual products.

The stats button shows you how much your commission is for each sale and the promote button generates a HopLink that will link your site to the vendor's. This is the link that you will have to use in your site; if you simply copy the URL of the vendor, you will not be credited with any traffic you drive to the vendor.

Such a simple process has seen them grow tremendously and they are one of the more preferred affiliate vendors in the market.

When compared to online stores, they also offer much higher commission rates, meaning you earn more. The difficulty though is in you making the sale. Everybody knows Amazon and is comfortable with purchasing from them. When they have to give out their credit card details in other places though, many people will refrain from doing so meaning that you will find selling that much more difficult.

Going with the products that have a number of affiliates is a good place to start off. The more the number of affiliates, the more the chances are that that particular product is a large selling one. This is a different take on aping your competition, and your whole strategy is based on the simple fact that if everyone else is selling something, and making a profit out of it, then you can as well.

Yet, this logic is not without its pitfalls. Just because a particular product has a number of affiliates, it is no guarantee that you will be able to sell the same product. It also means that the competition is already stiff, and breaking into the market may not be easy.

Moreover, all the juicy sounding URL addresses would have already been taken which will make it more difficult for you to get the product name into your address. This is especially true if you are going for a totally unrelated product from what you are selling now, or are starting out new.

The other way is to look at the products with the maximum commission and then figure out a way of driving sales. Unfortunately this is easier said than done, and in many cases the commissions are high and the competition low because making a sale is so difficult.

The second thing that you will have to think about is that you can drive any amount of traffic to a particular site, but unless the home site is written well, no one is going to buy the product. For example, if you become an affiliate to sell eBooks for someone else, no matter how well you do your part, unless the home site itself has something that will make the people you send buy the product, you are not going to get any sales, and all your effort will be wasted.

Generally speaking going for the sure shot ones, like the ones that have a lot of competition is better, because if you work hard enough and get the ranking on your site up, you are at least guaranteed success. If you go for the hard to sell products, you cannot be sure that even after all your effort you will make any sale.

Promotional tools

Many times the affiliate site will offer all the promotional tools that you need, like page banners, informative articles, and even email promotions. Of course, the articles cannot be used as is but you at least have all the basic information about the product to help you create a wonderful sales pitch. If you find a seller that does not do this, it is better to stay away from them. This is because it shows that they are not serious about marketing online. It also means that you will have to put in that much more effort at marketing their product and their commission may not justify this added effort.

Use keyword tools

Most search engines offer free keyword tools that you can use to find related keywords. There are also other paid software programs that will help you do the same thing, but with increased functionality. While usually these tools are used mainly to find related keywords, they are also useful to find the most often searched strings.

This process is time consuming but will give you solid information to move forward on. For example, if you feel that washing machines are a good option, just typing washing machines into the tool will give you all the related search strings that are being searched for, their local and global numbers for the month.

This gives you an approximate idea of the number of people searching for a particular product. For example, if you type in Yorkshire Terriers, you will get a number of results that range from more than 80, 000 to less than 2,000. You therefore know that there are at least 80,000 searches for the Yorkie on average every month. On the other hand, if you put in Labrador retrievers, you will find that this number triples. It is pretty obvious that there are more people searching for them than for the Yorkie.

This gives you a good baseline to start from. While looking in online stores like Amazon may give you similar data there are two advantages of using the keyword tools that search engines offer.

First, you get actual numbers of the number of people searching for a certain product while all Amazon can do is tell you which products sell the most. Since you are more interested in promoting products that sell more, you may be losing out on a good opportunity to convert sales.

Amazon gives you data for sales converted, while Google gives you data about potential for sale. There may be innumerable reasons why there may be more people searching for a product than there are buying it, and one of them could be that the sellers are not doing a good job. This gives you the opportunity of entering a market where even if there are other competitors, the competition is really nothing much to talk about.

The second advantage is that Google offers you the ability to find niches that are as yet untouched. While this may be difficult and may take a lot of time, the possibility at least exists with Google, while with any other way this possibility is not an option at all.

Of course, doing random searches will mostly be a waste of time. You will have to approach it in an systematic manner. The way to do this is to brainstorm and note as many niches as you can come up with. Then go through Google with all these niches one by one. If you hit something, that's good, if not continue the process.

Because this process is so time consuming many people profor to go with tho affiliato notworl(or ohool(on onlinc stores. Yet, doing this is still not useless. If you do get lucky and chance upon a niche where there are a number of people searching, but very few people selling, you are on to a sure thing.

Chapter 6 - Go for the basic needs

While there are countless products that you can sell, it is better to categorize these products into which are considered needed, and which are not. Usually the amount of up sell you have to do for those products that are basic necessities is not too great while if you want to sell a luxury item, you might have to do a lot of up selling.

The margins are more in luxury goods, but the sales are much greater in basic goods. While it is easy to get swayed by the high profit margins of luxury products, if you are a newcomer it may be a better idea to go with low cost, but easy to sell goods.

While food, clothing and shelter are considered the basic needs for all life, with regards to Internet marketing it is a little different. When you look at products to market go with those that are related to wealth, health, and relationships.

Wealth

If you go to any search engine, usually the most searched for string will be something related to making money. Because some people are lazy by nature, this will be narrowed down to making money online. Many people consider this niche to be an almost sure thing, because of the propensity of people to be fooled into making a quick buck.

There are innumerable sites that market eBooks that give expert knowledge on how to make money easily online, and although the sales of these books are not explosively high, they are high enough for a new entrant to think that he or she has a good chance, even if the competition is really stiff. There are pitfalls though, and you have to ensure that you choose a good book to market. The only way for you to find out if the book is any good is to buy and read it, which will increase your initial costs quite a bit.

If you compare the different books you have identified with their sales numbers and page rank on Google, you may be able to narrow down your search, but even there, you will never know what you are selling until you try it out yourself.

Books are not the only thing, and there are a number of blogs that are dedicated to giving you tips on how you can make money online. If you plan to enter this niche, you are almost guaranteed success, as long as you put some effort into delivering a unique product. This is simply because of the competition out there, and while finding a truly unique product may not be easy, you can manage to do quite well if the design of your page is appealing, and the content good.

This does take effort, but if you manage to get the right combination, it is a perennial source of income for you. This niche never flags, and there is interest year round, and especially with the economy not doing too well, it looks like more and more people want to make money easily online.

You do need to do a little bit of homework though, and make sure that the home site that sells the book is also a really good one. There is no point in you driving traffic to another site just to see it all wasted with you getting very little sales to show for all your efforts. Another thing you need to be wary of is a site that advertises for other things besides the main product.

There is every chance that this product is an ad for which the owner is paid, and by driving traffic there, all you are doing is helping somebody else get richer.

Health

This is the second niche where you are sure to hit success. The whole world is worried about health nowadays, and not only because it affects the quality of their life, but because health care has become quite expensive. What with social security and medical insurance looking for ways to wrangle out of paying for expensive treatment, it looks like it is a good idea to stay healthy.

The problem is that many people either do not have the time to exercise, or do not have the inclination. The majority fall into the latter category. This is the reason why any site that gives effective, weight loss remedies without the person having to do anything is sure to become a success.
There are various sub niches in health, like fitness, running, weight training, apart from the evergreen weight loss. Many people tend to go with the fitness niche simply because there are quite a few products to sell in this niche like supplements and pills.

As long as you manage to get your rankings high enough, you are sure to make a minimum of a few sales every month, and as long as you are not depending on one product alone, but are spreading it out a bit in the form of four or five different products, you can get a combined income that is quite a reasonable sum.

Unfortunately, just as in any other niche that is popular, this also means that you will have to spend a lot of time on updating your site. There is no way you can sit back after you do your initial work because your rankings can plummet in a short time if you do not add content to your site.

Getting a ranking high enough for you to see some activity and even some money is not an easy thing. Retaining your high ranking is even more difficult because you will have to constantly fight off efforts by newcomers who want to topple you. Yet, it is a lucrative market, and if you do manage to get into the top three or five results, you are sure to make much more money than almost any other niche.

Doing the homework is therefore essential. Just pumping your site full of content or into article directories and back linking alone is not enough. Search engines are evolving much faster than we can keep up with them, and 10 times out of 10 they are able to identify a good site based on a combination of factors. Many of these factors are a closely guarded secret, but it is imperative that you make sure that your site follows all the norms that search engines look for. Concentrating on one or two alone is not enough.

In addition, the search strings that are being used are never static. While one month a particular string may be at the top of the list, the next it may be a totally different one. This means that all your content will either have to be reconfigured to reflect this change, or new content added. A simple example would be to go to Google AdWords and type in any niche that you like. "Washing machine" is searched a maximum of 1,830,000 while Labrador 2,740,000 times. Health is searched 45,500,000 globally, and even related keywords are looked for more often than the primary keywords in other niches.

Relationships

Relationship is another niche that is quite lucrative. This niche is a little more difficult to target, as there are any number of combinations of primary keywords, which is why they are not as popular as the previous two.
Yet they still offer possibilities, and if you are interested in relationships or have a lot of experience, this may be a good niche to choose. People are always looking at ways to make relationships work or even to get back into old or broken relationships. Many are indeed so desperate that they will try almost anything, because this niche does not satisfy a physical, but an emotional need.

There are few negatives for this niche except that sales are not easy to come by. There is a lot of freely available information on the net about relationships, and people do not find it necessary to pay for a product when they can find it free elsewhere.

This does not mean that you cannot earn money in this niche; on the contrary, it is one of the three most successful niches you can choose.

Chapter 7 - Other Considerations

Once you have identified the product that you want to market, there is still a little bit of work to do. and they are set out below.

Profit

This is obviously the first thing that you should look for in any product that you want to market. Affiliate marketing is a business, and just as in any other business, it is profits that matter. All decisions therefore come down to this baseline, and if you, after all the research in the world find that the product is not profitable, there is no point in going any further.

This is the reason why there are a number of people who started out with affiliate marketing, but had to give up half way, because there was no money to be made. This is also the main reason why newcomers are advised to go for those products that are already selling well. That way there is not much decision making regarding the product to go with. You will have to concentrate only on improving your ranking in

Google and while the competition is also much stiffer, you will at least know that if you can't sell, it has nothing to do with the product.

It is important to make a distinction between profit and profitability. Most people go with high profitability, which means that you get high margins on sales. While this may be a good income stream, it may be a good idea to take a look at the low margin, high volume segment. Many times the quantity of sales will be such that your total profits will be more in the low margin products than in the high margin ones.

For example, trying to sell an eBook for $60 a book may give you a commission of $5 per sale but if you are netting only 20 sales a month, you are only earning $100.
Instead, if you go for the ones that sell at $10, your commission may well be only $1, but if you are able to make 200 sales, you earn $200. This is only an example but it serves to illustrate the point.

Marketability

The first point dovetails into this. You need to find products that are marketable. Unless there are people to buy what you have to sell, there is really no point in you even trying to sell it. You need to make sure that there is a market for your product before you try to sell it.

There may be geniuses who were able to create a market, but this rarely happens. For the vast majority of us, selling products that already have an existing market is the only way to go.

Stick to consumables

This is good advice because only consumables are sure to give you repeat sales. For example, dog food may not sound appealing, but there are more than 1,500,000 people searching monthly for it, and they will have to buy dog food the next month and the month after that. This way, even if the size of the market is low, you are guaranteed recurring sales because as long as you give a good deal, buyers will return to you.

Of course there is always the fear that repeat customers will go straight to the home site, but your advantage as an affiliate is that you are not stuck to just one product. You can have as many brands as you wish and as long as you make sure that there is something different about your site, like a new brand that you feel is better, or something else, people may very well try out different products from you. It is easier to remember just one site and bookmark it, rather than 10 different ones for 10 different products, and so you are ensuring that they will keep coming back to you first before going elsewhere. As long as they do that, you will be credited with the sale.

Quality

This is important because although the net gives you a lot of anonymity, purchasing is still governed by old fashioned values like quality of the product. You are putting your reputation at stake by saying that a product is good quality, so either be sure that the product really is as good as it says it is, or give an honest review. Either way you will have to try the product to build up consumer confidence in your site.

It is not necessary that you sell only top quality products. High quality generally means high price but more people are satisfied with fairly high quality and a lower price product. Just don't say that something is really good when it is not.

For example, if you are selling cameras, there are a number of low cost, good enough cameras that will probably make up the bread and butter of your sale. You cannot afford to not sell them as the high priced ones sell much less. Yet, you need to make sure that the purchaser gets good value, so inflating specifications, and giving opinions like something is really great when it isn't, should be avoided.

Honestly saying that something is good only for a certain use, and that if you want more functionality you should go with another model, is more appreciated than if you say that it is the best that money can buy.

Many sites offer customer reviews as their marketing ploy thinking that a customer who finds a review by another customer will be more inclined to believe it. Unfortunately, not all customers leave a review, which means that many of these sites resort to putting in reviews under different names just to bolster their site. This also means that you will have reviews that are not entirely accurate, meaning that you yourself are bringing down the value of your site.

A much simpler and effective way is to just give an honest review and as long as you have taken the time to review the product properly, you will find people respect your opinions. This may take longer, but in the long run, is more profitable.

Popularity

Look into the popularity of the product first. Affiliate marketing is not as easy as just creating a site and becoming an affiliate. A lot of legwork is needed and just because you find a product that is searched for does not make it a good niche to be in.

For example, there are a large number of people who search for anything "Labrador". Yet, this is of no use to you because most of these people are looking for information. Few people buy puppies online, and although you have the option of marketing various dog products, it is still not a very profitable niche to be in. Even people who like their dogs very much generally get what they need at the supermarket, and unless you can offer a really good deal on your products, they will not buy it.

This is just an example of something that is really popular, but does not net you anything in the form of money. Of course, if this is a niche you really want to be in, you could do further analysis on finding out why exactly people do not buy, and then create a site that takes into account all these problems. This is not only time consuming and expensive, there is also no guarantee of success.

Chapter 8 – Conclusion

We have discussed a number of different way in which niches can be identified, products chosen and how to conduct the basic research into doing this. Unfortunately, because affiliate marketing is so dynamic, and relies on a number of different things, not just the product, it is not always as easy as you think. Just increasing the page rank does not depend on only one factor, but many different ones, and when you include marketing a product into the mix, it gets much more complicated.

Affiliate marketing is the way to the future, especially if you do not have products of your own to sell. Most sellers are more than happy to have as many affiliates as possible, because it just means that they are increasing their sales that much more. The money paid out in terms of commission is nothing compared to what they will earn through you.

Anyone who has done affiliate marketing will tell you that it is not easy. While you can afford to relax a little after you have a stable set up, you will always have to watch trends to ensure that you are not left out when they change. For example, if you are selling clothing online, there is huge potential for it. Last year alone saw a 15% jump in online sales of clothes and this continues rising. Yet, you will have to ensure that you stay ahead of the curve here, as if what you sell is out of fashion, your high page ranking is not going to help you.

Depending on the kind of niche you choose and the product you go with, you will have to make small changes to the strategy to give you the best returns. There are also a number of unexplored ways of not only choosing a product to sell, but also to sell it better, and newer techniques are constantly being adopted. Making money by selling affiliate products is easy only for those who are already set and can afford to experiment.

For those of us who are starting out, it is the best way to start out with a very small investment.

ABOUT THE AUTHOR

IQ Press, Inc. is a small publishing company dedicated to providing access to educational materials primarily in small business start-up and development. Their mission is to bring the reader useful information that can be implemented with a small capital outlay and generate income streams for the reader to implement.

We trust that you will enjoy these reports and that they will help improve your life.

To get a jumpstart in online marketing download our exclusive quick start guide here: www.IQPress.org/Quickstart

REFERENCE MATERIALS

Other books you may enjoy to help you on your journey:

Affiliate Marketing for Beginners. Have you heard about affiliate marketing but not quite sure if it's real or really works? This definitive guide will lay out the ins and outs of this interesting field. Filled with tips and hints, it also has information on what to look out for.

Affiliate marketing truly can be started with very little money and has the potential for great rewards. Simple to start with the right guidance, affiliate marketing seriously reduces the risk in starting your own business. Imagine a business with little investment, no inventory, no customer service, no shipping and handling and no risk! Further it can grow to replace your current income and still be operated as a part-time operation. All you need is the enclosed information and you're ready to start.

Affiliate Marketing Secrets: You did become an affiliate marketer to become rich, right? OK, so now what? Start here and learn how to take your fledgling affiliate marketing company to the next step. This report is packed with secret tips and tricks to help you grow your company quickly. After all, your goal is to add customers and new products quickly and expand your business without taking on more risk.

In this short read you will find dozens of ideas to help move your company forward. Not a bunch of theoretical ideas but actual tested tips and techniques to move you towards your goal quickly.

Affiliate Marketing and Success Systems: This report is a compendium of tips and ideas to help keep you on track with your affiliate marketing business. You want an automatic money machine? We'll show you not only how to grow but also to get that growth on autopilot! With a few simple programs you can get the company to generate a continuous income stream. That's why you went into this type business, right?

Using this report will turbocharge your results and help you simply and effectively grow your sales. Bring in a constant stream of new customers and new products to offer your existing customers for a generous income. You could even quit your job if you wanted! Imagine all that free time while still enjoying a great income.

Available exclusively at: www.IQPress.org

www.ingramcontent.com/pod-product-compliance
Lightning Source LLC
LaVergne TN
LVHW052314060326
832902LV00021B/3891